A WORLD OF STEAM

by

Nils Huxtable

Publication Data

© 1996 by Nils Huxtable
Published by Steamscenes
2254 Lawson Avenue
West Vancouver, BC V7V 2E4
Canada
Printed and Bound in Canada by Hemlock Printers Ltd.
ISBN First Printing – May 1996
ISBN 0-9691409-5-9

Acknowledgements

The author would like to thank the following people who have helped, directly or indirectly, to make this book possible: Bill Alborough (To Europe for Steam), Dusty and Christine Durrant, Mike Fox, Dave and Hazel Fleming, Chris Garnett, Joachim Hild, David Ibbotson (Dorridge Travel), Charlie and Mellie Lewis, Tim Murray, John Middleton (Steam and Safaris), Geoff Monks, Dennis Moore, Gunter Oczko (Steam Loco Safari Tours), Chris Skow (Trains Unlimited Tours), Manfred Stolz, Ivor Thomas, David Thornhill, Mike Tyack, Reggie Tonry (World Rail Travel Specialists), Ad van Sten, Wayne Weiss and Richard Weston. Special thanks to Perry Boeker, Stuart Gear and Peter Madliger of Hemlock Printers Ltd.

Dedication

For my parents, who enabled – and encouraged – me to explore a world of steam.

Frontispiece

CHINA   Jiamusi shed, in the Northeast, had an allocation of RM Pacifics for passenger duties on all four lines radiating from that city. Possibly the cleanest, best-kept RM left in the country by February 1989 is getting a rub-down. A few Chinese engines carried safety or work efficiency slogans; this one is decidedly political: "Hold the red banner high. Advance with courage."

To the railway enthusiast, the whole world is a railway map.
Spreading out over the globe, a vista of gleaming metal trails beckons him invitingly to
prospects of new sights and the fascinatingly unfamiliar shapes of masses of metal in motion.

– E. S. Wolff, *The Railway Album*

INTRODUCTION

A Saturday afternoon in July. It has been raining steadily for the past few days. In the grey twilight, clouds gather around the Outeniquas. I can almost hear a Garratt climbing towards the summit with the Cape Town-Port Elizabeth passenger, but that was years ago . . .

I am just in time: the 14:15 from Knysna is whistling as it comes off the branch. Rolling in to Platform One, the 19D uncouples and moves forward to the water column. Apart from the shouts and cheers emanating from the Signalman's Arms – it is the World Cup rugby final – George station is deserted. Weeds sprout from the platform canopies, one of the footbridges (formerly for non-whites only) has been roped off, and the v-shaped name boards reading "George – Junction for Knysna" are illegible. The semaphores have been removed from their brackets, and trains are now radio-controlled from Oudtshoorn. Nowadays, the only through passenger service on the Garden Route is the weekly "Southern Cross". The Knysna branch has become a museum line.

As I stroll the length of the platform, the 19D clanks past, turns on the triangle and backs down to the coal stage, where tubs are pushed around an oval of track and their contents dumped clattering into the tender. After one last tubful of coal, the 19D couples onto a 24 Class 2-8-4 and shunts it into position, ready for Monday morning. Then, it will be a different story: there will be more passengers, train crews, carriage cleaners, more activity and noise, and for a while George will regain some of its former steam atmosphere.

The echoes of the "Dolly" reverberate against the buildings. Then the Signalman's Arms erupts, and the 19D's whistle blows again and again. South Africa has won the championship.

It is, of course, a mistake to return and expect things to be the way they were. This is not the South Africa of 1972, when there were more than 2,000 operating steam locomotives, or of 1955, when I received my first railway book as a Christmas present. Entitled *The Railway Album* by E. S. Wolff, it contains a painting of a 23 Class 4-8-2 steaming through the Karoo with the "Union Limited" (later renamed "The Blue Train"). Perhaps that book, worn with childhood use and still on the shelf, has served as an impetus for this one.

During the 1950s, my trainwatching activities included the "Red Dragon", "Capitals United Express" and "South Wales Pullman", together with local passenger workings and holiday relief trains observed near Llansamlet on the Swansea-London main line. Another childhood haunt – Felin Fran, a goods yard on the Swansea District line, provided still more variety, with Irish boat trains and empty stock workings, as well as milk, parcels, fish, steel coil and coal traffic.

The railway scene at home was entirely steam: "Castles", "Counties", "Halls", "Granges", "Manors", "Britannias", and a host of 2-8-0s, 2-6-0s and tank engines. Even now, forty years later, some of the names are as fresh as the day I first saw them: *Defiant, Spitfire* and *Morning Star.* Then came *The Railway Album.* Perhaps because they were so different from my familiar favourites, the foreign engines – studied intently on rainy afternoons – were also imprited on my memory: a "Josef Stalin" 2-8-4 steaming through a blizzard at night; a New Zealand Government Railways' K Class 4-8-4 crossing a steel trestle; a Canadian National 4-8-4; a Rhodesian Railways 12th Class 4-8-2; an East African Railways 4-8-2+ 2-8-4 Garratt and a Nacionales de Mexico 2-6-6-2. A world of steam!

My fascination with railways – and steam in particular – was heightened by visits to my grandparents in Switzerland. In those days, train travel across Britain and much of the Continent was a steam adventure: a "Castle" would take my parents and me to the whistle-filled bustle of London Paddington; a Bullied Pacific drew our train to the Kentish Coast; and after the Channel crossing, a relay of SNCF engines shrilled through the darkness, covering us with cinders on the long night journey across northern France. At an early age came the realization that steam's appeal knows no frontiers.

I had only just started my locospotting career when the decision was made to emigrate: to California. I "copped" the Bullied Pacific that brought us to Southampton – No. 34001 *Exeter*, and ironically, the last steam locomotives I saw in 1957 were American: two ex-U.S. Army 0-6-0 tanks shunting the docks, glimpsed from a porthole on the S.S. *United States*.

For a young steam enthusiast, relocation to California was a sobering experience. For if I had ever imagined a place *without* steam, this was it. The Southern Pacific Railroad, visible from our front door, had dieselized a few months previously, and it was not long before the U.P.'s Big Boys and Challengers, too, were set aside, along with Colorado & Southern 2-10-2s, Illinois Central 4-8-2s, Nickel Plate 2-8-4s and Norfolk and Western articulateds and 4-8-4s. Aged ten, I didn't stand a chance of getting to them in time.

So began my independent travels, financed at first by indulgent parents, then by various part-time jobs. Homesick for steam as much as for friends and relatives, I returned to Britain beginning in 1961, where steam withdrawals were already occurring at an alarming rate. Within a matter of months, my beloved "Castles" were decimated. Finally, by 1967, I could bear the run-down of British steam no longer, so I crossed the Channel once more – for an appointment with French and German Pacifics, and the huge broad gauge 4-8-4s of Spain. A few literary aids helped: a little magazine called *European Railways* and articles in *Trains* magazine entitled "Jet Search for Steam". As well as studying for college exams, I spent my time planning summer holiday itineraries with *Cook's Continental Timetable*. Postgraduate studies? To New Zealand, for 4-8-2s on the "South Island Express"; Australia, where Pacifics still hauled the "Newcastle Flyer". Then on to Indonesia, Malaysia, Thailand, Taiwan and Japan, with its double-headed "Niseko Express" 4-6-4s and triple-headed 2-8-2s. But the high point of my first round-the-world trek was that most memorable of train journeys: the "Rossiya" from Khabarovsk to Moscow and a first encounter with the Soviet Railways' green, red and cream P36 4-8-4s. At last, the pages in the "Overseas Railways" chapter of *The Railway Album* were coming to life.

Soon, however, an element of desperation began to turn what had begun as a hobby into an obsession. For the steady decline of steam worldwide made it difficult to know where to go next. Czechoslovakia, in time to see the blue 498.1 Class 4-8-2s? South Africa, before the wires went up on the Bloemfontein-Kroonstad line? South America? India? No matter where I traveled, I would be too late for a particular class of engine or steam-operated stretch of railway somewhere else.

Today, millions of miles and many countries later, the Age of Steam is almost over. And it is time to share some of the images accumulated over a thirty-year period. In doing so, I offer them as a tribute, not only to steam locomotives, but also to the railwaymen and women who operated, maintained and repaired them, and to the people who depended on steam as a means of transportation, and in many instances, as a source of water and fuel. For them as for me, steam was a way of life.

Unfortunately, colour photography is a limited medium. No picture can convey the experience of riding a Baldwin 2-10-2 across the Bolivian altiplano at night. Or of camping at the lineside while 4-8-4s broke the stillness of the starlit Karoo with chime whistles and sharp, staccato bark. Or of sitting above the cowcatcher of a Guayaquil & Quito 2-8-0 as it blasted through rock cuts and tunnels below the Devil's Nose. Or of watching in awe while the steam from two QJ 2-10-2s – and a third, pushing – blotted out the sky at thirty-five below.

Of course, the pictures presented here reflect personal preferences. I can only hope the reader will derive as much enjoyment from perusing these pages as I have found in traveling around the world in search of the steam locomotives that as a boy I used to dream about.

As the 25NC 4-8-4 accelerates, a persistent tugging accompanies each piston thrust. A hint of sulfur wafts through the corridors; cinders rain down on the carriage roofs, pelt the windows and cover the floor. Whistle shrieking, the big Henschel races into the twilight, trailing a long smudge of smoke against the yellow sky. Crackling like cannon fire, the engine's exhaust beats become a roaring storm of noise – a low-flying jet fighter. Beneath the swaying coaches, rail joints and switch frogs rattle and click, receding in metallic ripples on a silver stream of steel.

Too soon, the brakes go on: Hamilton, where nearly a quarter of a century before, I photographed double-headed 4-8-4 condensers on freights and Pacifics on suburban trains. Finally, the brooding slums of Bloemfontein, once the steam capital of South Africa. In 1972, there were more than 200 steam movements each day, and a pall of coal smoke, visible for miles, hung over the city. Now, the station is silent, the Victoria Hotel, where the nocturnal exertions of 4-8-2s threatened to bring down the walls, closed. A chapter, too, is closing, and as yet another steam journey ends, I cannot help but wonder if this one will be the last.

Nils Huxtable
West Vancouver, BC
Canada
May 1996

► SOVIET UNION   Of the Soviet Railways' P36 Class 4-8-4s, the late P. B. Whitehouse, railway author and photographer, wrote: ". . . winter was the most dramatic time to travel, with the train ice encrusted amid a landscape of endless snow and stark leafless trees – then came the curves with a view ahead and a plume of pure white steam, as the P36 thundered on . . ." Red wheels coated with ice, P36 0189 has just taken over from a classmate at Skovorodino, and in a few minutes, the Moscow-bound *"Rossiya"* will be departing for Yerofey Pavlovitch, in December 1972 the western-most limit of steam operation for this and other through passenger trains on the Trans-Siberian.

◄ EAST GERMANY   One of the last steam sheds in East Germany was Halberstadt, where a number of 50.35 Class 2-10-0s were allocated until the end of regular standard gauge steam operations. Of the 350 Deutsche Reichsbahn 50 Class 2-10-0s remaining in the Soviet Zone of Germany after World War II (total constructed: 3,141), 208 were rebuilt with new, all-welded boilers, combustion chambers and Heinl feed-water heaters. A decade before the final run of revenue service DR standard gauge steam (made by one of these engines), No. 50.3570 was having its smokebox cleaned inside the roundhouse. March 1978.

► PORTUGAL   The metre gauge lines of northern Portugal featured a wonderful steam collection, from 2-6-0Ts and 0-4-4-0T mallets to Henschel 2-8-2Ts. The Douro valley was served by four metre gauge branches, two of which, the Corgo and the Sabor, were worked by mallet compounds with the unusual 2-4-6-0T wheel arrangement. Overnight, moisture from the river has formed a heavy frost on the tracks. With Train 6411 from Regua to Chaves, a 2-4-6-0T mallet shuffles along, unfolding a cloud of smoke and steam. December 1973.

◄ INDIA   On India's railways, the pace of broad gauge dieselisation and electrification eliminated steam some five years earlier than originally projected. Withdrawals included the modern WP Pacifics, former stars of the main line. Just months before retirement, No. 7184 departs Ludhiana with local train 4LJH to Jakhal. The class prototype came from Baldwin which, along with the Canadian Locomotive Company, Floridsdorf, Chrzanow and Chittaranjan, supplied 755 of these bullet-nosed 4-6-2s. January 1994.

► SOUTH AFRICA   Specifically-assigned crews kept their engines in immaculate condition and often decorated them with nameplates and ornaments. Prestige locomotives assigned to railtour duty received the same attention: brass fittings and copper pipework on 19C 4-8-2 No. 2439 are polished to a high gloss at Oudtshoorn. July 1990.

◀ POLAND   Last stronghold for the Polish P8 4-6-0 was the town of Międzyrzecz. The Polish Railways (PKP) had 430 Okls on hand at the end of World War II; only five were left by 1980. From the fireman's side, a view along the boiler barrel of Okl 296, heading west with the 15.35 to Rzepin on August 17, 1979.

▶ SOVIET UNION   A design dating from Czarist times, the S/Su 2-6-2 was the standard Soviet passenger engine, complete with safety railings mounted on the running boards and front end. Described as "the greyhounds of the Russian railways", they hauled branch line locals, commuter trains and expresses. One of their last top-link assignments was the *"Leningrad Express"*, which this Lithuanian Railway 2-6-2 will take as far as Grodno, on the Polish border. No. 251.83 rides the turntable at Vilnius in April 1975. A few months later, the engine was scrapped.

◀ ZIMBABWE   At the same time that the National Railways of Zimbabwe was having Garratts upgraded at Zimbabwe Engineering Co., Bulawayo, new diesels were also arriving. A sunrise view of the motive power transition shows a GE DE 10 occupying the main line at Tajuntunda, while a 15th Class 4-6-4+4-6-4 has taken the siding; both with coal empties for Wankie Colliery. July 1991.

▶ BELGIUM   In 1985, Belgium – as well as Germany – celebrated 150 years of railways. Two SNCB steam locomotives – a streamlined 12 Class 4-4-2 and a Canadian-built 29 Class 2-8-0 – powered special trains that summer. Here, the fireman of No. 29 013 prepares for departure at Menen. This engine, built by MLW in 1945 as one of 300 North American 2-8-0s ordered by the Belgian National Railways, had the distinction of heading the last regular steam train in the country, in December 1964.

◄ INDONESIA   The ultimate tender mallets built for Java, the CC50 2-6-6-0s held on until 1984, working the Cibatu-Garut branch. By August 1983, the most spectacular section to Cikajang had been abandoned because of the unsafe condition of the bridges and the inability of the ageing mallets to tackle the four percent grades. On July 5, 1981, No. CC5003 is having no trouble with a two-coach train on level track near Garut. On October 28, 1984, No. CC5001, the first of the thirty compound 2-6-6-0s built by Werkspoor and SLM in 1927-28, was the last to be withdrawn.

► INDIA   In their declining years, the South Eastern Railway's WP Pacifics were responsible for some local workings and even the *"Tirupati Express"*, although they presented a sad contrast to their top-link status of a decade previously. As the morning sun begins to penetrate the murk hanging over Gondia, a signalman updates his logbook. Meanwhile, a WP, its skyline casing removed for ease of maintenance, leaves with a stopping train for Nagpur. January 1987.

◄ U.S.A.   Southern Pacific *"Daylight"* GS-4 4-8-4 No. 4449 helped bring about a steam revival in the western U.S. Removed from a Portland city park and overhauled for the American Freedom Train in 1975, the stream-styled Northern became a familiar sight on the main lines of its former owner during the 1980s and early 1990s. Portland-bound with an excursion returning from Sacramento's second Railfair (in May 1991), No. 4449 battles unassisted through a late Spring snowstorm between Andesite and Grass Lake, California.

► SOUTH AFRICA   On July 30, 1991, it was announced that with the end of regular SAR steam operation, the George-Knysna branch had been selected as a museum line. This picture attempts to show why. A few minutes prior to the passage of the morning mixed to Knysna, a light mist has crept across the far shore of the lagoon at Sedgefield, creating a canvas for this silhouette of 24 Class 2-8-4 No. 3622. July 1983.

◄ GERMANY   Taken out of traffic in 1972, the sole surviving Saxon XII H$_2$ *"Rollwagen"* 4-6-0 was back on the scene as an active museum engine less than a decade later. During a *Plandampf* centred on Aue in April 1993, No. 38.205 was assigned to passenger service on the Chemnitz line. At the south end of Aue station, the engine takes water after uncoupling from its train.

► TURKEY   The mountainous section of the former Smyrna Cassaba Railway was worked by 565-series *Kriegslok* 2-10-0s and Prussian G10 (TCDD Class 55) 0-10-0s. Doubleheading was the rule over the 157½ miles from Alasehir to Afyon, which included many tunnels, viaducts and a grade of 1 in 40. In February, 1977, Train 1161, the 06.10 Alasehir-Afyon mixed, leaves Konaklar behind Nos. 55051 and 55017. This is the beginning of the climb to the Anatolian plateau.

► U.S.A. On the slopes of Mount Shasta, California, wind whips the snow into a white frenzy. In nearby McCloud, however, protected by stands of Ponderosa pine, 2-6-2 No. 25 (Alco 1925) is being readied for a snow excursion. As if on cue, the fireman enters a scene once commonplace when steam was king on the McCloud River Railroad. February 1984.

►► SOUTH AFRICA Among the important contributions to steam development in later years was modified 25NC Class 4-8-4 No. 3450. Reclassified 26 and nicknamed the *Red Devil*, the engine incorporated a number of improvements resulting in greater power output and increased efficiency. From the dirt road paralleling the Kimberley-De Aar main line, the one-of-a-kind 4-8-4 was panned doing about 60 miles per hour north of Potfontein in July 1983. This, the all-stations De Aar-Kimberley, was the sole remaining main line steam passenger train on South African Railways until the re-introduction of limited steam working on the *"Trans-Karoo"*, *"Trans-Oranje"*, *"Amatola"* and *"Algoa"* expresses in 1989/90.

◄ ECUADOR   On the Guayaquil & Quito Railway, the five percent grade into the Andes began at Bucay, and a Baldwin 2-8-0's exertions demanded frequent stops to replenish the tender's limited water supply. With the loss-incurring railway under constant threat of closure, even a scene as mundane as this could not be taken for granted. August 1992.

► CHINA   The Baotou-Lanzhou main line through northwest China provided one of the world's great steam shows. Climbing out of the Yalu River valley on the edge of the Gobi desert, westbound trains had to negotiate four horseshoe curves between Zhongwei and Gantang. Freights were double- and, occasionally, triple-headed, and on frosty winter days, the plumes of steam and smoke from three trains – each on a different section of the grade – would be visible at one time. A snow-storm has softened the barren landscape, the mercury reads -25° Celsius, and two QJ 2-10-2s are slogging into the first horseshoe. December 1991.

◄ U.S.A.   During the 1980s, a North American steam renaissance saw twenty preserved main line engines – from a 4-4-2 to two articulated types – returned to operation. Between Bonsack and Webster, Virginia, Norfolk & Western A Class 2-6-6-4 No. 1218 is nearing Blue Ridge summit with a ferry move from Roanoke to Alexandria. Heavy rains have turned the fields to streaks of silver, and the roofs of farm buildings gleam in the morning light. Tragically, Norfolk Southern discontinued all steam excursions at the end of 1995, and retired No. 1218 a second time. October 1989.

▲ SOUTH AFRICA   Described by A.E. Durrant in *Twilight of South African Steam* as "the most remarkable narrow gauge express passenger locomotives ever built", the six 16E Class large Pacifics supplied by Henschel in 1935 had six foot diameter driving wheels (the largest fitted to any narrow gauge steam engine), the heaviest axle load of any SAR locomotive, rotary cam poppet valves, and a boiler and grate that in three-foot, six-inch gauge terms looked – and were – huge. The 16Es were latterly stationed at Bloemfontein for passenger diagrams to Noupoort and Kimberley until withdrawal in 1972. Maintained in working order for specials, No. 858 takes water and has its fire cleaned at De Brug in July 1990.

◄ GUATEMALA During the 1960s, roundhouses full of outside-frame 2-8-0s and 2-8-2s, spindly steel trestles and mixed trains attracted aficionados of three-foot gauge railroading to the former International Railways of Central America, originally built and operated by the United Fruit Company. Long after most FEGUA steam had been scrapped, a steam freight could still be arranged. To the bemusement of bystanders, 2-8-2 No. 205 (BLW 1948) smokes through Escuintla station on August 24, 1987.

► GERMANY A blizzard has almost buried the rails of the Cranzahl-Kurort Oberwiesental narrow gauge line. Train 6909, the 08.09 from Cranzahl, has fallen behind schedule because of drifting snow. The sound of its arrival muffled by a curtain of snowflakes, 2-10-2T No. 099.757, brake pump panting, stops short of Hammer-Unterwiesental station so that the guard can clear the points. February 1993.

◄ AUSTRIA Closed in 1982, the Steyrtal-bahn, Austria's oldest 760 mm-gauge railway, was an ideal museum line, although only the Garsten-Grünburg section survives. In happier days for the enthusiast (though not for the ÖBB, which considered the line a hole in its pocket), 0-6-2T No. 298.25 leaves Leonstein with the afternoon passenger train from Garsten to Mölln, on the portion now closed. Where else could one find a station named Unterhimmel-Christkindl? December 1974.

► WEST GERMANY The German Federal Railways (DB) had planned to take its remaining Prussian P8 4-6-0s out of service by 1971. Two years later, however, Nos. 038.382, 711 and 772 were still working local and limited-stop passenger trains (and even the occasional freight or ballast turn) between Tübingen, Horb, Böblingen and Hausach. At sunrise on this Spring morning, No. 038.382 starts away from Eutingen with Train N3935, a local for Stuttgart. May 1973.

◄ SOUTH AFRICA   During the early 1970s, Bloem-fontein was one of the world's busiest steam locations, with a hundred steam movements each day. Seen from a distance, the city would appear on the horizon as a smudge of coal smoke. By 1976, however, following dieselisation of the line to Springfontein and electrification to Kroonstadt, Bloemfontein shed – and steam's occupancy – had been cut in half. Despite the explosive effects of a dozen sets of safety valves blowing off at regular intervals, this July 1983 scene cannot compare to the one featured as a double-page spread in *The Great Steam Trek*.

▶ INDIA   In many parts of the developing world, the steam engine served as a kind of mechanical Prometheus, bringing fire – and hot water – to people living along the railway. At Jalandhar shed, young women search for partly-burned fuel among the ashes left by a WL Class 4-6-2. January 1994.

◀ CHINA   In Winter, the roundhouse at Changchun was like an arctic cave. A fog of accumulated steam from the locomotives inside impeded visibility, and portions of the concrete floor, plastered with ice, were extremely hazardous. As the shed pilot, JF Class 2-8-2 No. 2422, stands by to retrieve an SL 4-6-2 from one of the stalls, a shedman opens the doors to the deep freeze. February 1989.

▶ BOLIVIA   A lonely stretch of metre gauge railway links La Paz with Argentina, and for the villages on the altiplano, the arrival of a train was always an important event. The silence of a windless afternoon is broken, not by a pan flute, but by the whistle of Baldwin 2-10-2 No. 705, pulling away from a water stop at Huari (elevation: 12,000 feet) with the weekly Uyuni-Oruro pick-up freight. By nightfall, locomotive, crew and photographer will have covered the 313 miles from Tupiza to Oruro in just over 36 hours. October 1976.

◄ PAKISTAN   By February 1988, all line work from Rawalpindi had been dieselised, and the only steam activity consisted of a few shunting turns and the occasional excursion. At dawn, while two freshly-painted and decorated *"Great Central"* SGS Class 0-6-0s are being coupled to their special train, the grimy station pilot presents a more accurate picture of steam in decline on the Northwest Frontier.

► CHINA   'Down on their hands and knees' was the enthusiast's expression for scenes like this: three QJ 2-10-2s – two on the front and one at the rear – exert their combined maximum of 9,000 horsepower as they struggle towards the summit between Liushu and Nancha, in northeast China, with a train of logs from the Wuyiling branch. The second QJ is lost in steam seeping from the lead engine. Filling the sky, the exhaust will linger in layers on the frozen air, then turn to ice crystals that sprinkle down like fine sand. December 1994.

◄ GERMANY   Two 86 Class 2-8-2Ts were required for working the sparse service on the Schlettau-Crottendorf branch, in the Erzgebirge region of Saxony. They remained in use until 1987, the last full year of standard gauge Deutsche Reichsbahn steam. One of these engines, No. 86.1001, became a regular performer at *Plandampf* events. Clear skies have turned ominous by early morning, and the embankment at Stenn furnishes a silhouette of this Zwickau-Falkenstein freight; doubleheaded 86 1001 and 50 Class 2-10-0 No. 50.1849 are darkening a sunless dawn. October 1993.

▲ HUNGARY   An award-winning design introduced in 1924, the mixed traffic 424 4-8-0 was one of five Hungarian State Railways (MÁV) steam classes still at work during the early 1980s. As late as 1987, a few 424s were available for ballast turns, diesel failures, tourist specials and breakdown trains. Leaving Papa on July 27, 1979, No. 424.173 passes an Austrian-style home signal.

◄ INDIA The railway infrastructure of Pakistan and India included a profusion of British-style semaphores. At the east end of Jalandhar station, all signals are at "danger". Meanwhile, a WL 4-6-2 slips on wet rails, its exhaust eclipsing the sun. January 1994.

► FINLAND During the 1970s, most remaining VR steam locomotives came to life only in Winter, when the ports were ice-bound, and extra traffic moved by rail. Summer was a quiet time for steam: although Kouvola's roundhouse was full of Trl Class 2-8-2s in August 1974, only one could move under its own power, ostensibly on stand-by for working freight to Kotka and Pieksamäaki. The roof gives a pigeon's eye view of the turntable, occupied by No. 1074. That year, 109 VR steam engines were still in stock; of these, seventy-nine were serviceable.

◄ CZECH REPUBLIC   During the night, another cold front has brushed across Austria and Bohemia, powdering the fields and dusting the trees. In the mountains, it is snowing still; the sunshine and blue skies around Kajov are merely a break in the weather. Assisted at the rear by 433.0 Class 2-8-2T No. 433.001, red, white and blue-liveried 477.0 Class 4-8-4T No. 477.043 leads a special from Česke Budejovice to Volary. The ČSD 477.0s were the world's most modern tank locomotives. Built between 1950 and 1955, these three-cylinder engines incorporated a welded boiler and firebox, mechanical stoker, Kylchap exhaust system and roller bearings. With smoke deflectors, skyline casing and a huge centred headlight, these visually striking machines were nicknamed "Papoušek" (parrot) by their crews. February 1993.

► ITALY   Connecting and eccentric rods serve as footholds for last-minute running repairs to 625 Class 2-6-0 No. 100 at Trento shed. March 1993.

◀ BRAZIL   Until 1983, one of the quaintest railroad systems in the world – totalling almost 200 kilometers – remained unaffected by progress. All of the two-foot gauge VFCO engines were Baldwin-built, including 4-4-0 No. 21, seen from inside the ornate train shed at São Joâo del Rei. Preserved as a museum railway in 1984, the 16-kilometer section from Sao Joâo to Tiradentes was retained for special trains. October 1976.

▶ CANADA   The lightly-laid 44.3-mile branch line between Chipman and Norton, New Brunswick, was home to three ancient Canadian Pacific 4-4-0s until 1960, the last year of Class I steam operations in Canada. All three engines have been pre-served. At Weldon Crossing, on the Salem and Hillsborough Railway, No. 29 of Class A1e (built in 1887) gleams in the last brightness of the Autumn sun. October 1989.

▲ PARAGUAY   On rails embedded in the Pampa grass, the weekly *"El Internacional"* from Asuncion, swaying like a ship in heavy seas, has managed to reach Carmen, 335 km, with 36 km to go. On this trip, at least, the North British-built 4-6-0 has neither derailed nor run out of leña (wood fuel). However, the train is late as usual, and during a water stop, a herd of grazing horses overtakes. Named for Paraguayan president Carlos Antonio Lopez, in office at the time of construction, the FCPCAL remained as built – and entirely dependent on steam – until the end. October 1988.

▶ SOUTH AFRICA   Dieselised on September 26, 1982, the 278-km Maclear branch, in the Eastern Cape, ran along the base of the Southern Drakensberg and Stormberg ranges. In the final years of steam operation, 19D Class 4-8-2s, nicknamed "Dollies", worked the daily passenger train and all freight traffic. One of the most scenic lines in South Africa, it became a favourite among enthusiasts, and under threat of closure, it featured in many tour itineraries. Recreating a steam-era mixed. No. 2698 is almost lost in its own leaking steam as it pounds around a curve south of Indwe just after sunrise. July 1995.

◀ U.S.A.   When trains operated year-round over 10,200-foot Cumbres Pass, the frequent movement of plow-fitted locomotives and a flanger kept the tracks clear. After economy measures closed the line during Winter, a rotary would be called out to reopen it. Little has changed since then. Between Chama and Cumbres, three 2-8-2s and rotary OY have spent two days removing seven months' accumulation of snow and ice. East of Los Pinos, the plow extra, with two Mikes shoving, becomes toylike against the snowscape. May 1993.

▶ INDIA   At stations and in railway yards, water columns also served as public bathing facilities. As women and children attend to personal hygiene at Ambala, a run-down WG 2-8-2 wheezes past. January 1994.